DATE DUE

MR 1 3 9			
JA 9 - 12			

Demco No. 62-0549

Hello Squirrels!

Scampering through the Seasons

by Linda Glaser ~ illustrated by Gay W. Holland

M Millbrook Press   Minneapolis

To my dear friend Jeanne,
who plants countless
seeds of kindness. _ LG

To my daughter and son-in-law,
Laura and Barry Uden,
with much love and gratitude. - GWH

Text copyright ©2006 by Linda Glaser

Illustrations copyright ©2006 by Gay W. Holland

Millbrook Press
A division of Lerner Publishing Group
241 First Avenue North
Minneapolis, Minnesota 55401 U.S.A.

Website address: www.lernerbooks.com

Library of Congress Cataloging-in-Publication Data

Glaser, Linda.
Hello, squirrels! / by Linda Glaser; illustrated
by Gay W. Holland.
p. cm.
ISBN 13: 978-0-7613-2887-2 (lib. bdg. : alk. paper)
ISBN 10: 0-7613-2887-4 (lib. bdg. : alk. paper)
1. Squirrels—Juvenile literature. I. Holland, Gay W., ill. II. Title.
QL737.R68G68 2006
599.36'2—dc22   2005003692

Manufactured in the United States of America
1 2 3 4 5 6 — JR — 11 10 09 08 07 06

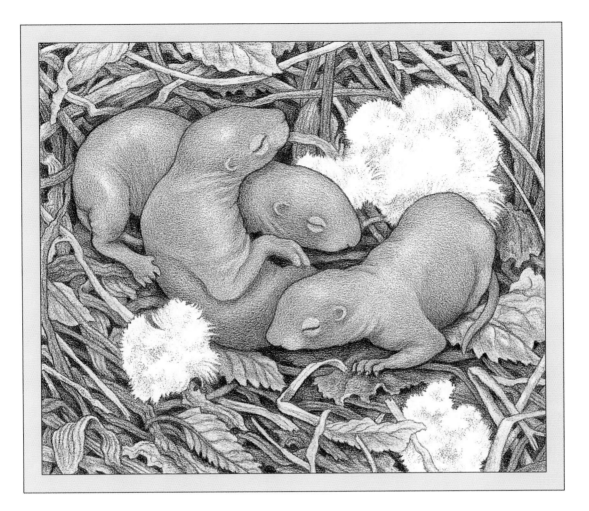

Hello baby squirrels
—just born in spring.

High up there in a round leafy nest,
you're so tiny and new, all pink and helpless.

Layers of feathers and grass and moss
cushion your nest so it's cozy and soft.

Mama squirrel feeds you milk and carefully licks you clean. She stays with you day and night . . .

. . . and only leaves the nest to eat.
She nibbles tender tree buds,

and new spring shoots,
leafy twigs, and bulbs and roots.

Mama fiercely guards you from strangers.

She moves you to safety, one by one,
when she senses danger.

As you grow, Mama leads you out
into the shaky world of trees.

Single file—steady, steady—
soon you'll learn to scamper, climb, and leap.

Hello noisy gray squirrels—
chit-chit-chattering in the leafy summer trees.
Finding food isn't easy in summer.

You can't find nuts or seeds,
so you eat mushrooms and twigs,
and you gnaw the bark of trees.

I love your bushy tail.
You use it in so many ways—

an umbrella in the rain . . .

and for shade on hot days—

for steering and balancing when you leap and climb and
oops!—like a parachute, puffed out just in time.

By now in late summer, you're each fully grown,

living in a leafy round nest of your own.

Hello busy squirrels
—burying nuts in the fall.

Your furry coat and tail are growing thicker.
You feast on fruits and nuts and seeds,
getting fat for winter.

You scamper, leap, and sail through the trees
and roll and tumble in fallen leaves.

You play tag, you chase and run
and switch who's "it" just for fun.

But the icy cold of winter will soon be here.

So you build warmer nests in the V's of trees
with plenty of sticks and moss and leaves.

Hello lively squirrels—
soaring through winter trees.

You furry gray acrobats leaping up there,
you add life and grace to the winter trees and air.

You search and dig up buried food,
even under deep snow,
scattering footprints as you go.

You find your own nuts and each other's nuts, too.
But *some* nuts aren't found by any of you.
Some stay buried and hidden, just waiting for spring.

At night, you sleep with your tail fluffed and thick
all circled around you—a warm winter blanket.

Furry gray friend, are you dreaming of spring—
when some nuts that you buried will turn into seedlings?

And do you wonder, like I sometimes do,
how many trees you have planted?

And how many gray squirrel families
will someday be born high up in *your* trees!

Here are answers to some questions you may have about squirrels.

chipmunk

*flying
squirrel*

**How many kinds of
squirrels are there
in the world?**

There are about 270 kinds of squirrels.
They include tree-living squirrels such
as gray squirrels and red squirrels;
ground squirrels such as chipmunks
and prairie dogs; and flying squirrels.
All of them are rodents.

**How do gray squirrels
find buried nuts?**

Most scientists believe that squirrels
use their strong sense of smell to find
buried food. Recently, a few scientists
suggested that squirrels may remem-
ber where they hide their nuts. Either
way, it's remarkable that squirrels can
find food buried in the earth even
under a foot of snow.

**Do gray squirrels ever
hibernate?**

No. During a cold spell, they may
sleep for a few days, curled up in their
tree nests (called "dreys"). But gray
squirrels don't hibernate because they
need to eat every few days.

**How far can a gray
squirrel leap?**

They've been known to leap up to
20 feet (610 cm)—which is about
20 times their body length—not
including their tail. Try this:
measure your height and multiply
it by twenty. Measure that amount
on the sidewalk. If you were a gray
squirrel, that's how far you could leap!